Bringing Out the Potential of Children.

Gardeners Workbook

&

Garden Journal

Bringing Out the Potential of Children. Gardeners

Workbook
with a
Gardening Journal

ISBN 978-1-7751178-6-5

Cover Design: Patrice Porter

A Garden of My Own

Give someone some fresh produce and they will eat for a day.

Teach them to garden and they will never be hungry.

They can have food to eat for a lifetime

My First Garden System will be:

☐ Container Garden

☐ Raised Garden Bed

☐ Square foot Garden

☐ Traditional Row Garden

☐ Patch Gardening

☐ A Combination of Systems

My Garden Checklist
Have some early successes which leads to being a lifelong gardener.

☐ My garden spot gets at least 6 hours of sun per day.

☐ My garden spot is somewhat sheltered and out of the wind.

☐ My garden is away from any trees who's roots may compete for my garden soil and water.

☐ My soil is prepped and ready to grow.

☐ My garden is easily accessible.

☐ I have access to water and gardening tools.

My Garden Seed List

Considerations:

✓ What you like to eat

✓ How much space you have for growing

✓ Growing conditions

✓ Is it easy or hard to grow

✓ What can you realistically eat or preserve

Good for Beginners	Best Variety for you
Beets	
Carrots	
Lettuce	
Radishes	
Squash	
Tomatoes	
Cucumbers	
Beans	

My Garden Seed List

Seed Name	Best Variety for you

My Garden Seed List

Seed Name	Best Variety for you

Seed Packs

Store your empty seed packs here, for future referencing, in this simple

DIY Envelope

Instructions:

Step 1: Cut along solid black line

Step 2: Bring bottom edge up so it covers these instructions. Fold along dashed line

Step 3: Glue outside edges together ----→

This will form your envelope to store your empty seed packs in.

Seed Packs

Store your empty seed packs here, for future referencing, in this simple

DIY Envelope

Instructions:

Step 1: Cut along solid black line

Step 2: Bring bottom edge up so it covers these instructions. Fold along dashed line

Step 3: Glue outside edges together ----→

This will form your envelope to store your empty seed packs in.

Seed Packs

Store your empty seed packs here, for future referencing, in this simple

DIY Envelope

Instructions:

Step 1: Cut along solid black line

Step 2: Bring bottom edge up so it covers these instructions. Fold along dashed line

Step 3: Glue outside edges together ----→

This will form your envelope to store your empty seed packs in.

My Garden Plan
Traditional Row Garden

Fill in the seeds to be planted in each row. Keep in mind you want the shortest plants in front on the South side.

Tallest Plants
Shortest Plants

My Garden Plan

Square Foot Garden

Divide your garden into 1' x 1' squares.

Plant a different kind of vegetable, fruit, herb, or flower in each square. Use the "recommended space after thinning." Space plants evenly by subdividing each square into 4, 9, or 16 smaller squares.

My Garden Plan

Raised Bed Garden

Make your garden beds narrow enough that you can reach the plants in the middle. Suggested raised beds 3'x5' or 4'x4' (use a square foot gardening plan in your raised bed)

Plant the tallest plants on the north side of the bed (south in the southern hemisphere) so they don't shade the shorter plants.

Put trellises on the north edge for vining plants

My Garden Plan
Raised Bed Garden (continued)

My Garden Plan

Container Garden

Draw small representations of the plants you wish to grow in each of the containers below.

Remember not to over crowd them.

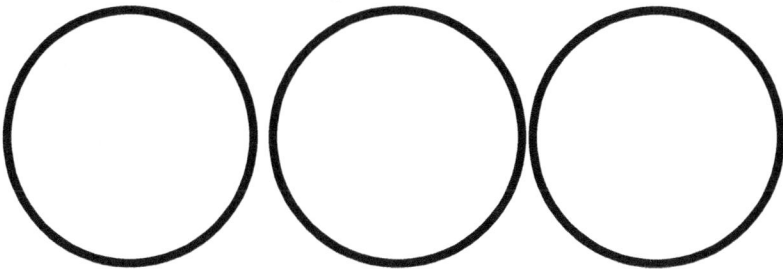

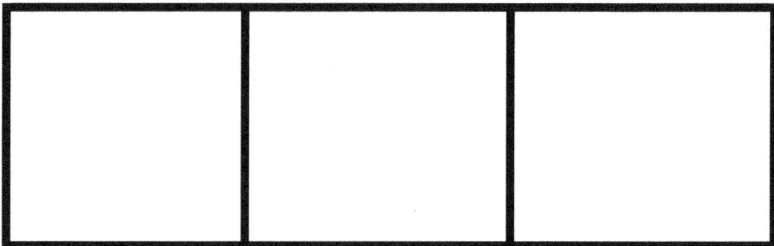

My Garden Plan

Patch Gardening

Can be used in mixed planting, or companion planting. Use a triangle template for group planting as in the hexagon pattern below. Tall plants on the north, shorter plants on south.

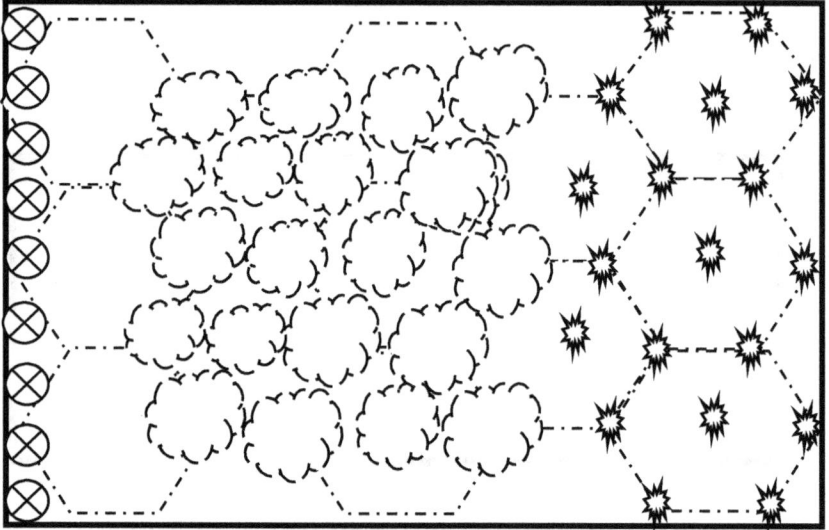

Sprinkle seeds over the entire patch trying to land the seeds about 1/2 to 1-1/2 inches apart. Cover with soil

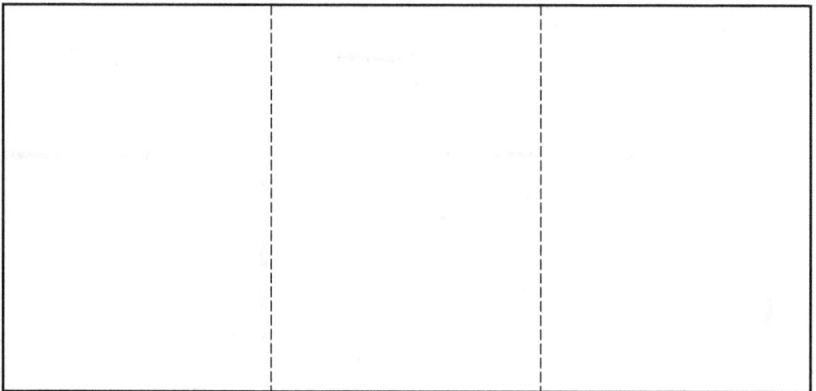

My Garden Plan
Make up your own planting design for a Patch Garden

My Garden Plan
Combined Planting Systems

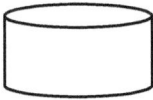

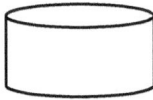

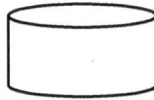

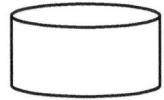

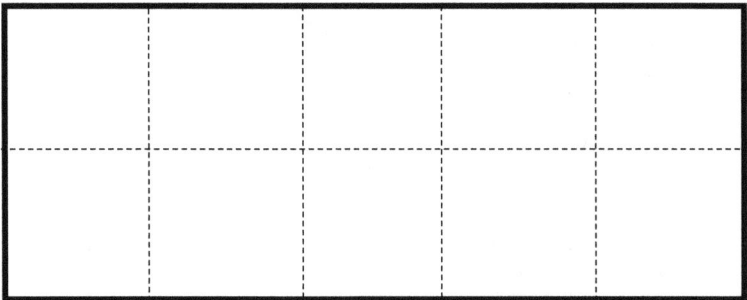

My First Garden

Garden Journal

Date _____

Temperature _____

Weather _____

What I did in my garden today...

_____

_____

I especially liked...

_____

_____

_____

_____

_____

Things to do...

_____

_____

_____

_____

_____

 My First Garden

Garden Journal

Date _____

Temperature _____

Weather _____

What I did in my garden today...

_____

_____

I especially liked...

_____

_____

_____

_____

_____

Things to do...

_____

_____

_____

_____

My First Garden

Garden Journal

Date _____

Temperature _____

Weather _____

What I did in my garden today...

_____

_____

I especially liked...

_____

_____

_____

_____

_____

Things to do... _____

_____

_____

_____

_____

 My First Garden

Garden Journal

Date _____

Temperature _____

Weather _____

What I did in my garden today...

_____

_____

I especially liked...

_____

_____

_____

_____

_____

Things to do...

_____

_____

_____

_____

My First Garden

Garden Journal

Date _____

Temperature _____

Weather _____

What I did in my garden today...

_____

_____

I especially liked...

_____

_____

_____

_____

_____

Things to do...

_____

_____

_____

_____

My First Garden

Garden Journal

Date _____

Temperature _____

Weather _____

What I did in my garden today...

_____

_____

I especially liked...

_____

_____

_____

_____

_____

Things to do...

_____

_____

_____

_____

_____

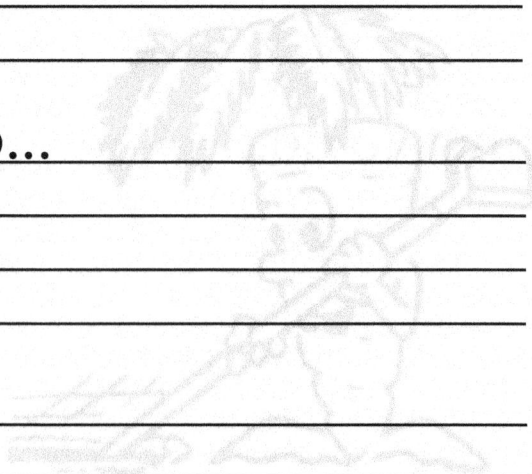

 My First Garden

Garden Journal

Date _____

Temperature _____

Weather _____

What I did in my garden today...

_____

_____

I especially liked...

_____

_____

_____

_____

_____

Things to do... _____

_____

_____

_____

_____

 My First Garden

Garden Journal

Date _____

Temperature _____

Weather _____

What I did in my garden today...

_____

_____

I especially liked...

_____

_____

_____

_____

_____

Things to do... _____

_____

_____

_____

_____

My First Garden

Garden Journal

Date _____

Temperature _____

Weather _____

What I did in my garden today...

_____

_____

I especially liked...

_____

_____

_____

_____

_____

Things to do... _____

_____

_____

_____

_____

My First Garden

Garden Journal

Date _____

Temperature _____

Weather _____

What I did in my garden today...

_____
_____

I especially liked...

_____
_____
_____
_____
_____

Things to do... _____

_____
_____
_____
_____
_____

 My First Garden

Garden Journal

Date _____

Temperature _____

Weather _____

What I did in my garden today...

_____

_____

I especially liked...

_____

_____

_____

_____

_____

Things to do... _____

_____

_____

_____

_____

My First Garden

Garden Journal

Date _____

Temperature _____

Weather _____

What I did in my garden today...

_____

_____

I especially liked...

_____

_____

_____

_____

_____

Things to do... _____

_____

_____

_____

_____

 My First Garden

Garden Journal

Date _____

Temperature _____

Weather _____

What I did in my garden today...

_____

_____

I especially liked...

_____

_____

_____

_____

_____

Things to do...

_____

_____

_____

_____

My First Garden

Garden Journal

Date _____

Temperature _____

Weather _____

What I did in my garden today...

_____

_____

I especially liked...

_____

_____

_____

_____

_____

Things to do... _____

_____

_____

_____

_____

My First Garden

Garden Journal

Date _____

Temperature _____

Weather _____

What I did in my garden today...

_____

_____

I especially liked...

_____

_____

_____

_____

_____

Things to do...

_____

_____

_____

_____

 My First Garden

Garden Journal

Date _____

Temperature _____

Weather _____

What I did in my garden today...

_____

_____

I especially liked...

_____

_____

_____

_____

_____

Things to do...

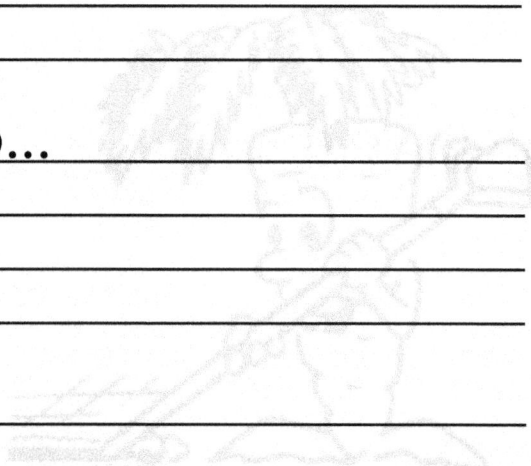

_____

_____

_____

_____

My First Garden

Garden Journal

Date _____

Temperature _____

Weather _____

What I did in my garden today...

_____

_____

I especially liked...

_____

_____

_____

_____

_____

Things to do... _____

_____

_____

_____

_____

My First Garden

Garden Journal

Date _____

Temperature _____

Weather _____

What I did in my garden today...

_____

_____

I especially liked...

_____

_____

_____

_____

_____

Things to do... _____

_____

_____

_____

_____

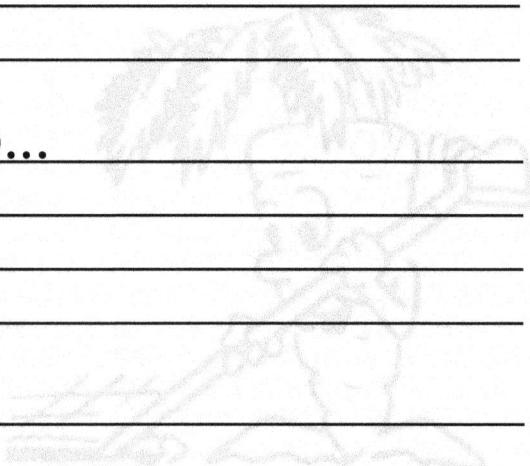

My First Garden

Garden Journal

Date _____

Temperature _____

Weather _____

What I did in my garden today...

_____

_____

I especially liked...

_____

_____

_____

_____

_____

Things to do...

_____

_____

_____

_____

My First Garden

Garden Journal

Date _____

Temperature _____

Weather _____

What I did in my garden today...

_____

_____

I especially liked...

_____

_____

_____

_____

_____

Things to do...

_____

_____

_____

_____

My First Garden

Garden Journal

Date _____

Temperature _____

Weather _____

What I did in my garden today...

_____

_____

I especially liked...

_____

_____

_____

_____

_____

Things to do...

_____

_____

_____

_____

My First Garden

Garden Journal

Date _____

Temperature _____

Weather _____

What I did in my garden today...

_____

_____

I especially liked...

_____

_____

_____

_____

_____

Things to do...

_____

_____

_____

_____

_____

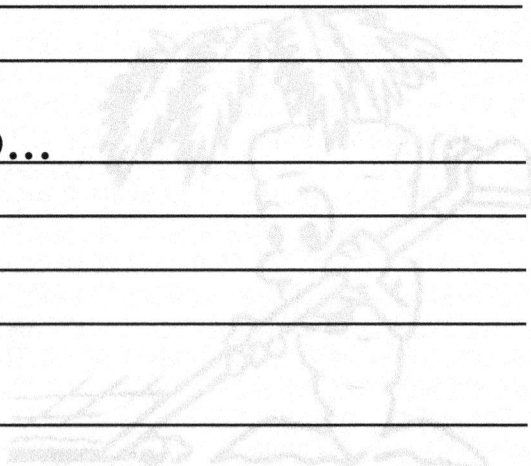

My First Garden

Garden Journal

Date _____

Temperature _____

Weather _____

What I did in my garden today...

_____

_____

I especially liked...

_____

_____

_____

_____

_____

Things to do...

_____

_____

_____

_____

 My First Garden

Garden Journal

Date _____

Temperature _____

Weather _____

What I did in my garden today...

_____

_____

I especially liked...

_____

_____

_____

_____

_____

Things to do...

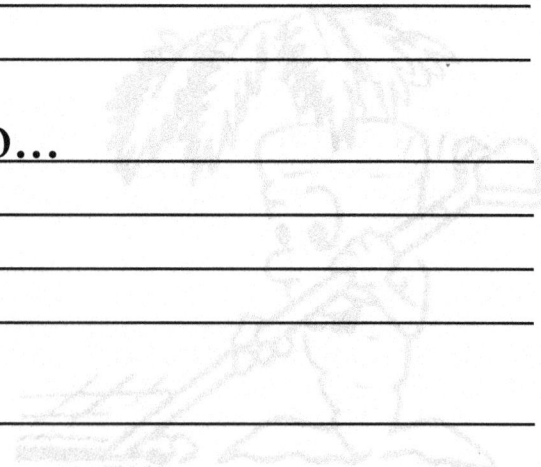

_____

_____

_____

_____

My First Garden

Garden Journal

Date _____

Temperature _____

Weather _____

What I did in my garden today...

_____

_____

I especially liked...

_____

_____

_____

_____

_____

Things to do...

_____

_____

_____

_____

_____

 My First Garden

Garden Journal

Date _____

Temperature _____

Weather _____

What I did in my garden today...

_____

_____

I especially liked...

_____

_____

_____

_____

_____

Things to do... _____

_____

_____

_____

_____

 My First Garden

Garden Journal

Date _____

Temperature _____

Weather _____

What I did in my garden today...

_____

_____

I especially liked...

_____

_____

_____

_____

_____

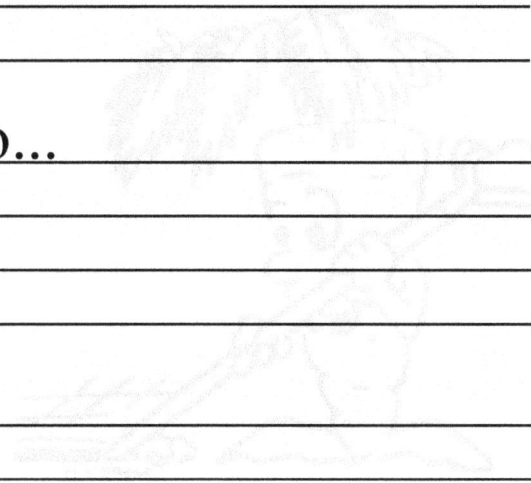

Things to do... _____

_____

_____

_____

_____

 My First Garden

Garden Journal

Date _____

Temperature _____

Weather _____

What I did in my garden today...

_____

_____

I especially liked...

_____

_____

_____

_____

_____

Things to do...

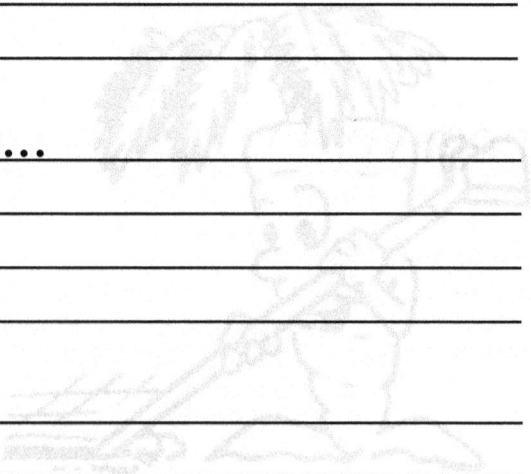

_____

_____

_____

_____

_____

 My First Garden

Garden Journal

Date _____

Temperature _____

Weather _____

What I did in my garden today...

_____

I especially liked...

_____

_____

_____

_____

_____

Things to do...

_____

_____

_____

_____

 My First Garden

Garden Journal

Date _____

Temperature _____

Weather _____

What I did in my garden today...

_____

_____

I especially liked...

_____

_____

_____

_____

_____

Things to do... _____

_____

_____

_____

_____

My First Garden

Garden Journal

Date _____

Temperature _____

Weather _____

What I did in my garden today...

_____

_____

I especially liked...

_____

_____

_____

_____

_____

<u>Things to do...</u>

_____

_____

_____

_____

My First Garden

Garden Journal

Date _____

Temperature _____

Weather _____

What I did in my garden today...

_____

_____

I especially liked...

_____

_____

_____

_____

_____

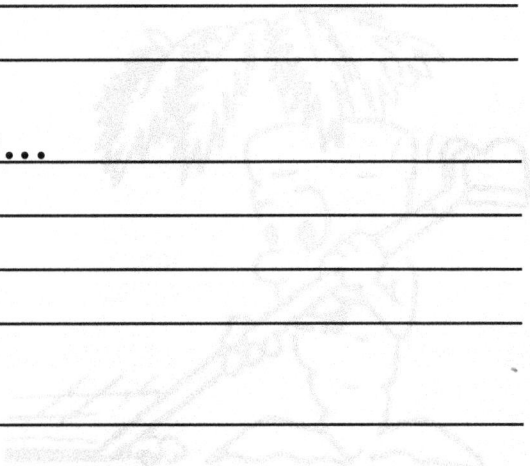

Things to do... _____

_____

_____

_____

_____

My First Garden

Garden Journal

Date _____

Temperature _____

Weather _____

What I did in my garden today...

_____

I especially liked...

_____

_____

_____

_____

_____

Things to do... _____

_____

_____

_____

_____

My First Garden

Garden Journal

Date _____

Temperature _____

Weather _____

What I did in my garden today...

_____

_____

I especially liked...

_____

_____

_____

_____

_____

Things to do... _____

_____

_____

_____

_____

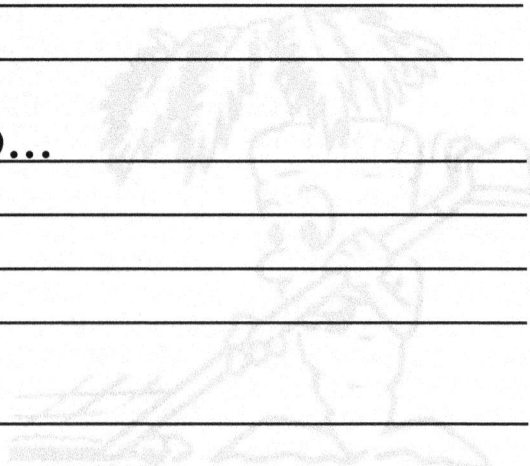

My First Garden

Garden Journal

Date _____

Temperature _____

Weather _____

What I did in my garden today...

_____

_____

I especially liked...

_____

_____

_____

_____

_____

Things to do...

_____

_____

_____

_____

 My First Garden

Garden Journal

Date _____

Temperature _____

Weather _____

What I did in my garden today...

_____

_____

I especially liked...

_____

_____

_____

_____

_____

Things to do...

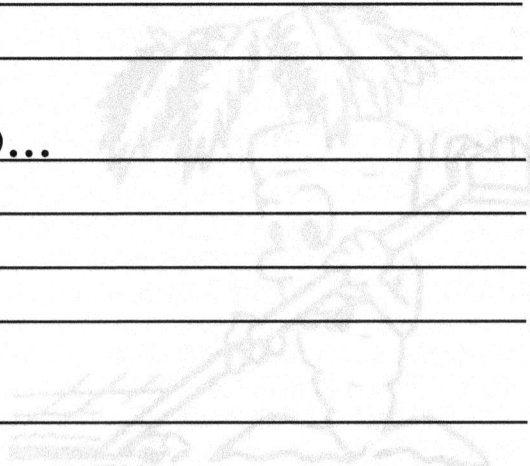

_____

_____

_____

_____

_____

My First Garden

Garden Journal

Date _____

Temperature _____

Weather _____

What I did in my garden today...

_____

_____

I especially liked...

_____

_____

_____

_____

_____

Things to do... _____

_____

_____

_____

_____

 My First Garden

Garden Journal

Date _____

Temperature _____

Weather _____

What I did in my garden today...

_____

_____

I especially liked...

_____

_____

_____

_____

_____

Things to do... _____

_____

_____

_____

_____

My First Garden

Garden Journal

Date _____

Temperature _____

Weather _____

What I did in my garden today...

_____
_____

I especially liked...

_____
_____
_____
_____
_____

Things to do...

_____
_____
_____
_____

 My First Garden

Garden Journal

Date _____

Temperature _____

Weather _____

What I did in my garden today...

_____

_____

I especially liked...

_____

_____

_____

_____

Things to do... _____

_____

_____

_____

_____

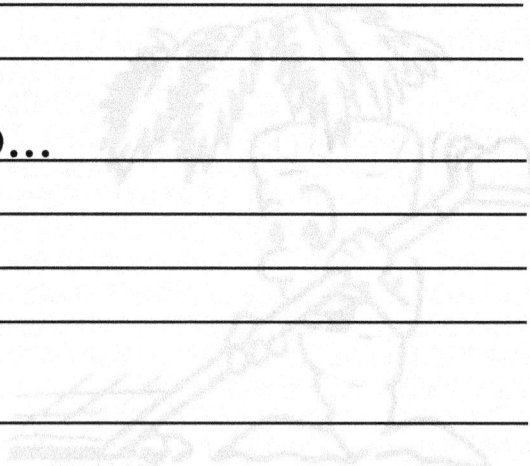

 My First Garden

Garden Journal

Date _____

Temperature _____

Weather _____

What I did in my garden today...

_____

_____

I especially liked...

_____

_____

_____

_____

_____

Things to do... _____

_____

_____

_____

_____

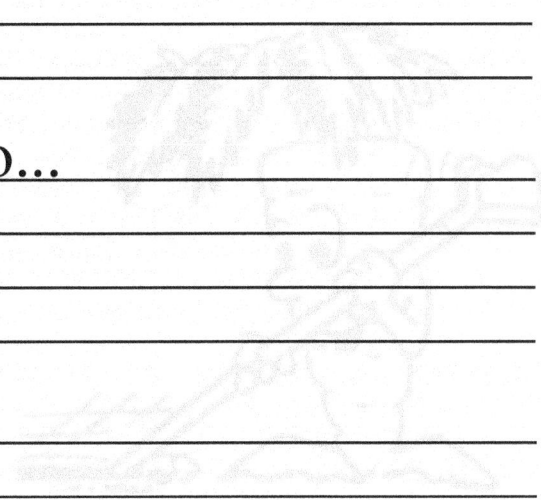

Notes

Notes

"The best way to have a good idea is to have a lot of ideas~ Dr. Linus Pauling

Notes

_____

_____

_____

_____

_____

_____

_____

_____

_____

_____

_____

_____

_____

_____

_____

_____

BRINGING OUT THE POTENTIAL IN CHILDREN SERIES

Volume 1 - Bringing Out the Potential In Children Writers/Authors

Bringing Out the Potential In Children Writers/Authors Workbook

Volume 2 - Bringing Out the Potential In Children Gardeners

Bringing Out the Potential In Children Gardeners Workbook

Volume 3 - Bringing Out the Potential In Children Cooks/Chefs

Bringing Out the Potential In Children Cooks/Chefs Workbook

Find them at the Full Potential Store – http://fullpotential.co.place

Amazon and other fine book stores.

www.ingramcontent.com/pod-product-compliance
Lightning Source LLC
Chambersburg PA
CBHW071932020426
42331CB00010B/2841